THE GEARHEAD'S GUIDE TO

BMX BIKES

BY LISA J. AMSTUTZ

CAPSTONE PRESS
a capstone imprint

Published by Spark, an imprint of Capstone
1710 Roe Crest Drive, North Mankato, Minnesota 56003
capstonepub.com

Library of Congress Cataloging-in-Publication Data is available on the Library of Congress
website.
ISBN: 9781666356595 (hardcover)
ISBN: 9781666356601 (ebook PDF)

Summary: Easy-to-read text and action-packed photos describe simple ways to modify and
improve BMX bikes.

Editorial Credits
Editor: Erika L. Shores; Designer: Heidi Thompson; Media Researchers: Jo Miller
and Pam Mitsakos; Production Specialist: Tori Abraham

Image Credits
Alamy: Lumi Images, 13; Getty Images: Trevor Williams, 23, Westend61, 19, yoshiurara, 15;
Shutterstock: Dmitry Kalinovsky, 7, Dmitry Niko, 17, Evgeny Karandaev, 12, Fabio Principe, 21,
J.A. Dunbar, 20, i3alda, throughout, design element, Lazor, 25, Marce | Clemens, 5, Melinda Nagy,
11, Mikbiz, 27, MISHELLA, Cover, Pavel1964, 8, PETER CLOSE, 18, Sergey Zaykov, 29, Skynavin,
10, Sue McDonald, 28

Printed and bound in the USA. PO4882

Table of Contents

Words in **bold** are in the glossary.

Tough Two-Wheelers

Racers line up at the gate. The starting gate falls. Bang! They're off!

BMX bikes take a beating. They twist and soar over jumps. They speed around curves. These bikes are small but tough. And you can make them even better with a few hacks!

FACT

BMX stands for bicycle motocross. The sport started about 50 years ago. Kids wanted to do motocross. They used bikes instead of motorcycles.

Make It Faster

Need more speed? Try making your bike lighter. One way to do this is to swap out parts for lighter ones. Start with the pedals, tires, seat, and bars. You can also use hollow stem bolts. They weigh less than solid ones.

FACT

A BMX race is called a moto.

You can shave more weight by cutting off extra metal. With an adult's help, shorten the seat post. Or trim the ends off long handlebars.

BMX racing tires can **accelerate** fast. The **tread** is small and knobby. Some riders like to use two sizes of tires. A thicker tire in front gives **traction**. A thinner one in back adds speed.

Racing bikes come with bigger **sprockets**. They make the bike faster.

Freestyle bikes have a smaller sprocket and driver. This gives more space for stunts. It lets the bike react faster.

sprocket

Think about how you use your bike.

Change your sprocket sizes as needed.

sprocket

A dirty chain can slow you down.
Tape two old toothbrushes together with
brush sides facing. Run the brushes over
your chain to clean it. Then slide a shoelace
through each link. This will remove more dirt.

Make It Stronger

Big jumps mean big air and big landings! Many riders like to swap **stock** parts for aftermarket ones. They can make the bike stronger.

Riders never want a flat tire. Do your tires have single wall rims? Swap them for double wall rims. They will last longer.

Freestyle bike frames are often made from **chromoly**. It is stronger than **aluminum**. You may want to swap out any non-chromoly parts.

Your bike's front fork takes most of the force on landings. A chromoly fork is safest. You may want to replace your frame and stem too.

FACT

BMX Freestyle is not a race. Riders do tricks on ramps, walls, box jumps, and spines.

Some bikes have front and rear brakes. A **gyro** comes in handy. It lets you do a **barspin** without tangling brake cables.

Here's a hack for your brakes. Make them grip better by rubbing a glue stick along the rim. You can rub soda pop on the rim too.

gyro

Make It Cooler

BMX bikes are pretty basic. But you can trick them out. **Decals** add style. Stripes, flames, and brand names are popular. Check bike shops or look online to find some you like.

Riders need goggles for safety. They can look cool too. They come in many styles and colors. Choose from clear, colored, or mirrored lenses. And don't forget your helmet! Show off your style with new decals.

FACT

A BMX race usually lasts 25 to 40 seconds.

Are your grips dirty or worn? New grips do not cost much. Pick a style and color you like. Add handlebar tape for even more color.

Grips can slip on dirt and oil. Use tape to clean the area under them. Just stick it on and peel it off. Now the grips will stay in place.

Pedals carry your weight. They need to be tough. You can make your pedals last. Choose one side to grip and one to **grind**. For metal pedals, remove the pins on one side. For plastic ones, mark one side with a pen or paint.

Colored rims and tires look great on BMX bikes. Try lighting up your ride with LED wheel lights. Add colorful spoke skins for even more flash.

Is your bike tricked out and ready

to roll? Ready, set, go!

Glossary

accelerate (ak-SEL-uh-rayt)—to speed up

aluminum (uh-LOO-muh-nuhm)—a lightweight metal

barspin (BAR-spin)—a trick in which the rider whips the handlebars around while in the air

chromoly (KROH-muh-lee)—a mixture of two metals called chromium and molybdenum

decal (DEE-kal)—a design printed on a sticker

grind (GRIND)—a trick performed by placing part of the bike on an obstacle and sliding along it

gyro (JYE-roh)—a part on the front of the bike that allows the handlebars to spin without tangling the brake cables; it's also called a detangler

sprocket (SPROK-it)—a toothed wheel that turns the chain of a bike

stock (STOK)—the parts of a bike installed by the factory

traction (TRAK-shuhn)—the amount of grip one surface has while moving over another surface

tread (TRED)—the pattern of raised lines on a tire or other object

Read More

Abdo, Kenny. *BMX*. Minneapolis: Abdo Zoom, 2018.

Carr, Aaron. *BMX*. New York: AV2, 2020.

Hale, K.A. *BMX Racing*. Minnetonka, MN: Kaleidoscope Publishing, Inc., 2019.

Internet Sites

How to Make a BMX Bike Faster
youtube.com/watch?v=yeIPu6wZ-zg

Riders: How-Tos
riders.co/en/bmx/categories

USA BMX
usabmx.com

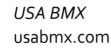

Index

About the Author

Lisa J. Amstutz is the author of more than 150 books for children. She enjoys reading and writing about science and technology. Lisa lives on a small farm in Ohio with her family.